This bite-sized book h
a useful overview of l
changing world and w
following:

- Understand how th
  it can have
- Appreciate the pros and cons of living in the era of
  artificial intelligence
- Embrace change in a positive and curious way
- Explore some of the core behavioural skills that will
  help you to thrive
- Be fit for the future and ready for anything

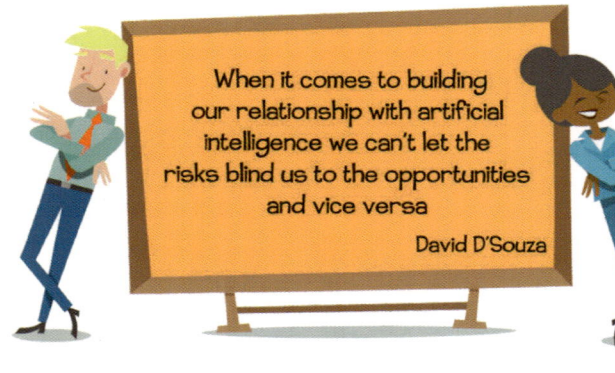

When it comes to building our relationship with artificial intelligence we can't let the risks blind us to the opportunities and vice versa

David D'Souza

Living with AI

Artificial intelligence (AI) is on track to be the most transformative technology in the history of humankind and we may find this a bit overwhelming and even daunting. Whilst it is uncharted territory and concerns have been raised about the impact it may have on humans, there will be many advantages to living with artificial intelligence. The benefits range from automating repetitive tasks, help making decisions, solving problems and saving us precious time.

There is a great deal for us to learn in this evolving industrial revolution and so much that we can benefit from too. Artificial intelligence has the capacity to unleash our human potential and create opportunities we have only imagined. As a tool it can help us achieve our goals, however it will only be a force for good if we use it responsibly and ethically.

Embrace change

Whether we like it or not, it is highly likely that the pace of change is only going to accelerate and, as the world evolves against the backdrop of the fourth and fifth industrial revolutions, then so must we. How well we respond and adapt to these changes will be highly dependent on the way we choose to behave – our humanness – and this will ultimately be the currency of our future.

One way to ensure that we are fit for the future is to be proactive and to continuously explore and nurture the behaviours that will help us to thrive. Outlined in this book are ten core behavioural skills that are highly relevant in the evolving 21st century and well worth cultivating.

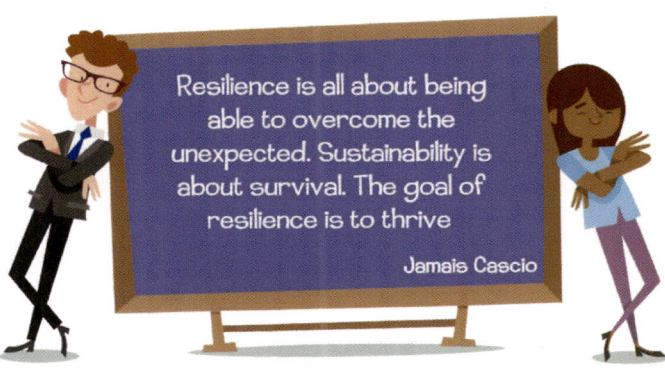

Resilience is all about being able to overcome the unexpected. Sustainability is about survival. The goal of resilience is to thrive

Jamais Cascio

1. Resilience

Human resilience, in many ways, is the foundational behavioural skill because it is about how we choose to respond in a dynamic and ever-evolving world. Let's face it, change can sometimes be a painful process and life has a way of throwing us a range of curve balls. How we respond to these challenges will define us and help us to build our strength and maintain our stamina.

Being resilient is not about "toughing it out" at any cost, sometimes to the detriment of our health. It is about looking after our overall wellbeing and pacing ourselves well, especially when we are under pressure. Continually building our resilience will help us to cope well with volatility, relentless change and uncertainty so we can build our strength, live a well-balanced life and thrive.

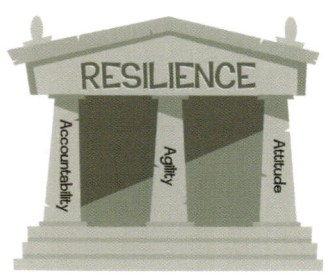

How to be resilient

1. Take personal responsibility
When we take responsibility for our own actions, we demonstrate accountability. It can be very liberating to acknowledge and understand that we can ultimately choose our response in every given situation.

2. Be agile and responsive
Agility is a key skill in the modern world where we need to think and act on our feet. This requires us to adopt a growth mindset and to be receptive to change and open to new learning and possibilities.

3. Maintain a positive attitude
With a positive attitude it is not about burying our heads in the sand. We will still be able to recognise the negative aspects of a situation; however, it then allows us to make a conscious decision to focus instead on the potential and opportunity in every given situation.

The art of life lies in a
constant readjustment
to our surroundings

Kakuzo Okakura

2. Flexibility

Living in a world that is in a constant state of flux requires us to be better at dealing with rapid change and to be flexible and responsive. Ultimately, agility and responsiveness are the keys to future success and a flexible approach allows us to adapt well and adjust to changing circumstances.

Challenging our own relationship and attitude towards change is a great place to start. If we get "stuck" in always doing things in the same way then we will always get the same outcome, which may not necessarily deliver the best results. As creatures of habit, we may not even be fully aware of what we do habitually on a day-to-day basis, so it is important to notice, challenge and flex our behaviours on a regular basis.

How to be flexible

TOP 3 TIPS

1. Take time to reflect
Building reflection time into our day is very helpful so that we can review what we are doing and make any necessary adjustments. If we always take the same approach, we are likely to get the same results; so, it may be time for some fresh thinking and a fresh perspective.

2. Change everyday routine
A simple way to start building our cognitive flexibility is to do everyday things differently. Even making the smallest of changes will help us to build and strengthen new neural pathways. We are essentially creatures of habit and we can, if we are not careful, get complacent and stuck in a rut.

3. Actively seek out new experiences
Seeking out new experiences has been shown to trigger the release of dopamine, a neurotransmitter that is commonly associated with our brain's pleasure and reward system. This feel-good chemical also enhances memory and our ability to learn, as well as helping us to stay more alert and on the ball.

A lot of people never use their
initiative because no-one
told them to

Banksy

3. Initiative

When we use our initiative, we ultimately empower ourselves because we do things without waiting to be told what to do. By being resourceful we find out what we need to know and do and this enables us to take advantage of opportunities that others may miss.

Using our initiative and resourcefulness can help boost our self-reliance, which is so powerful when it comes to getting things done. This, in turn, will increase our self-confidence and help us to perform better in the future especially in challenging and changing circumstances. It is important to remember that opportunities don't happen, we create them, and using our initiative is the springboard for getting great things done.

How to apply initiative

1. Be proactive
We can be proactive by anticipating what needs to be done and by doing it before being asked to do it. We can then use our knowledge to determine whether we have the skills and resources to make decisions on our own and if we need to get some additional support or guidance.

2. Be a good decision-maker and take action
Acknowledge that decisions are timely and there will be some occasions where we have to just bite the bullet and make our mind up, take action and accept responsibility for the consequences.

3. Be courageous
We may well act on our own initiative and we may not always make the best decision. This however, is all part of the learning process, and can help us to discover useful improvements. It is important to remind ourselves that we don't fail, we learn.

The bad news is that time flies.
The good news is that
you're the pilot

Michael Altshuler

4. Time management

Imagine if time was a bank account and each morning we were credited with 86,400 seconds. If, by the end of that day, we hadn't spent any of the credits then they would instantly be deducted from our account. What would we do? It is highly likely that we would make every effort to take care of those seconds and invest them wisely. It is interesting, though, how much time can be taken for granted and those seconds become lost or wasted.

We don't need to work harder, we need to work smarter! How we manage our time impacts on the quality of our lives, and as time is such a valuable commodity, we need to spend it well. It is however, our behaviours around our time management, that will have the most valuable impact.

How to be a good time manager

TOP 3 TIPS

1. Plan your day

Taking time to plan our days will also help us to keep focused and motivated because we will then be able to monitor what we have achieved. It will help us to feel more organised, calm and in control and better able to prioritise.

2. Schedule in rest time

Creating moments of sanctuary in our day, and scheduling in proper breaks, is a great way to re-energise and refocus. Going immediately from one meeting or task to another can be exhausting. It is far more constructive to take some time out to have rest stops, so we can clear our minds and be more productive.

3. Declutter

Creating an environment around us that provides more space, energy and clarity will impact on our health, happiness and overall wellbeing. The tidier and the more minimalistic we are, the easier it will be to locate things, and this can save lots of time.

Blessed are the curious
for they shall have adventures

Anonymous

5. Curiosity

Curiosity is about possessing a strong desire to learn, know and understand something new. When we seek out challenges and new experiences, we broaden our horizons. In many ways, curiosity is the catalyst of innovation and when we are curious, we have an ongoing, intrinsic interest in both our inner experience and the world around us.

Curious minds are active minds, and active minds become smart minds, and curiosity is associated with intelligence, creativity and problem-solving ability. Curious people seek out new experiences and are open to exploring fresh ideas and possibilities. The most valuable question that we can ask when we encounter anything new is "What can I learn from this experience?"

How to be curious

TOP
3
TIPS

1. Embrace diverse viewpoints

We work and share our lives with people from so many different backgrounds and across a wide range of age groups. Being curious rather than judgmental about differences will help us to expand our minds and expose ourselves to fresh viewpoints, values and beliefs.

2. Ask open questions

A curious mind is a probing mind and there is great benefit to asking open questions, for example: why, how, where, what, when, which, who? These types of questions open up opportunities to gain further information and avoid shutting down conversations with closed questions.

3. Actively listen

We need to be genuinely interested in what other people have to say and be fully present and listen with an open mind. It is important to be mindful of assumptions and judgments, so that we can fully absorb all of the information that is being shared without distraction.

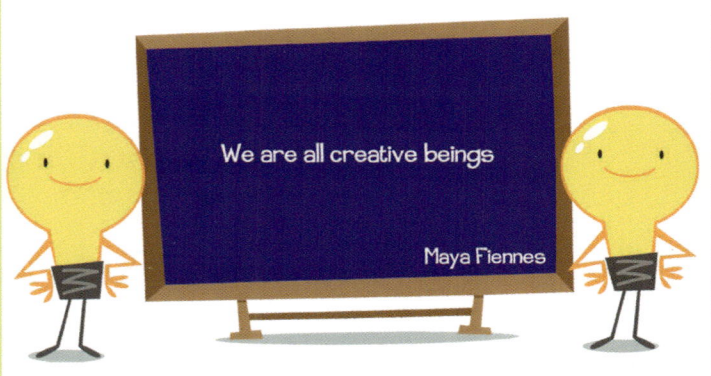

We are all creative beings

Maya Fiennes

6. Creativity

Creativity is about unleashing the potential of our mind to conceive new ideas. It is characterised by our ability to perceive the world in a different way and to make connections between seemingly unrelated phenomena, so that we can generate better outcomes.

Creativity is a useful tool for solving problems or for when we need to explore new and innovative ways of doing things. It is about seeking out new opportunities, to produce original ideas, and applying imagination and inventiveness. We are all creative beings and exploring some of the tools that are available to enhance our creativity is an excellent use of our time because creativity is one of the key employability skills of the future.

How to be creative

TOP
3
TIPS

1. Nurture a creative network
Working in isolation can stifle creativity and having a network we can reach out to and bounce ideas off is really important. Collaborating with others will also stimulate fresh thinking and unleash new ideas and innovation.

2. Stay calm and energise
The best neurochemical cocktail for our most creative work is a high level of both serotonin and dopamine. This combination of neurotransmitters will help us to feel both calm and energised. Practising mindfulness, eating a balanced diet, drinking water, sleeping well, exercising and resting will help us to be at our most creative.

3. Embrace being different
It is essential to maintain our individuality as creators. Some people may find our ideas outlandish and even attempt to suppress our creativity, however we mustn't let them stifle us. Creativity after all, is about being able to express ourselves, and our ideas in a different way.

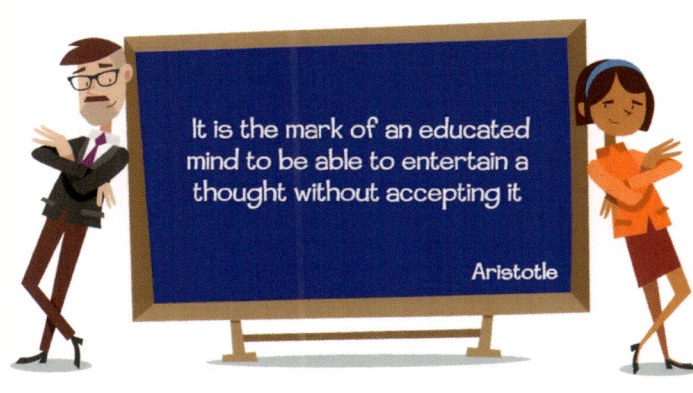

It is the mark of an educated mind to be able to entertain a thought without accepting it

Aristotle

25

7. Critical thinking

There is a big difference between knowledge and wisdom. Whilst we may acquire information, it's what we decide to do with that knowledge that is the real intelligence. We are living in the "information age" and with so much spurious information about we simply cannot take everything we come across at face value.

Critical thinking is a way of thinking in which we don't just accept everything we are exposed to and is the process of analysing, evaluating and rationalising information objectively. A good set of critical-thinking skills will help us to draw conclusions from a set of information and discriminate between what is useful and what is not. This, in turn, will enable us to be a better problem-solver and make well-informed and intelligent decisions.

How to be a critical thinker

TOP
3
TIPS

1. Be analytical
Applying analytical thinking begins with objectivity and relies on observing, gathering and evaluating evidence so we can arrive at a better-informed and more meaningful conclusion.

2. Be objective
Remaining as objective as possible when looking at information and focusing on facts and a thorough evaluation of the information at hand are essential. Being objective can be challenging, however making a conscious decision to step back from a situation will help us to see the bigger picture.

3. Pause and take time to think
One way to gain a better perspective of a situation is to pause and take some time to consider what is really going on. Very often we may feel that we are being pushed into reaching a conclusion before we have had sufficient time to apply critical thinking. So, ensure you have adequate time to think properly.

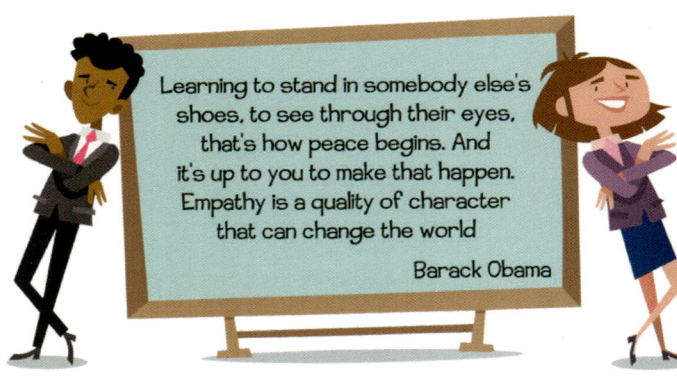

Learning to stand in somebody else's shoes, to see through their eyes, that's how peace begins. And it's up to you to make that happen. Empathy is a quality of character that can change the world

Barack Obama

28

8. Empathy

Humans are social beings, and we all have the capacity to develop empathy which enables us to build stronger and more supportive relationships. Like any behavioural skill, empathy can be cultivated through intentional effort and practice. Empathy is our ability to sense other people's emotions and understand how they may be feeling. It is about seeing things from someone else's perspective and imagining ourselves in their position.

Practising empathy helps us to connect and relate well with other people in our lives. By being empathetic we can better "read" another person's inner state and interpret it without blaming, giving advice, or attempting to fix the situation. Empathy ultimately improves human interaction and is one of the most valuable gifts that we can offer any other human being.

How to be empathetic

TOP
3
TIPS

1. Step into the other person's shoes
To practise empathy there is a very useful skill that can help called "perspective taking". This is about consciously putting ourselves in someone else's shoes and imagining what challenges they might be facing and how it could be making them feel, think and behave.

2. Be fully present
Being fully present requires us to make a conscious decision to give the other person our undivided attention. So, being aware of any potential distractions is important, as well as setting aside our own internal mind chatter so that we can focus on what the other person is saying.

3. Listen actively
Listening is one of the most powerful and constructive ways that we can demonstrate empathy. When we practise active listening, we are listening with purpose and with a deep desire to want to really hear and understand what someone is saying.

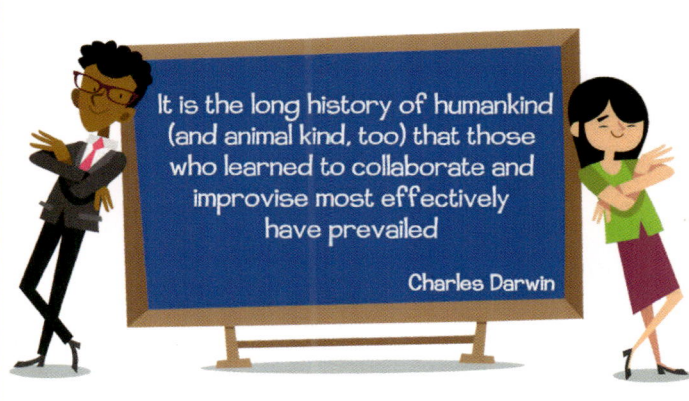

It is the long history of humankind (and animal kind, too) that those who learned to collaborate and improvise most effectively have prevailed

Charles Darwin

9. Collaboration

Collaboration is ultimately the art of co-operating and producing something with other people, whether that's with another individual or a team of people. Collaborating well with others and pulling together as a team with a common purpose can be highly motivating and help us to feel more energised and involved.

Working together provides a great opportunity to share experience and we can learn so much from each other, especially when we share our skills and strengths. Success when shared with others can be so much sweeter and so much more rewarding.

How to collaborate well

TOP 3 TIPS

1. Embrace collaboration

More and more in business the need to collaborate is being identified as a vital ingredient for success. Exploring and clearly understanding the benefits of collaboration are the first steps to being a great team member.

2. Be well organised

Collaboration is about co-ordinating well with others, so it is important to be well organised. If we are untidy and work in chaos this will hinder the progress of projects and also make things difficult for other people within the team.

3. Be appreciative

This begins with taking time to reflect on what other people are contributing and looking for opportunities to express our appreciation and gratitude. Sometimes a simple thank you can go a long way in helping to motivate people and we never know what impact it may have.

Creativity is thinking up new things.
Innovation is doing new things

Theodore Levitt

10. Innovation

In a nutshell, innovation is about how we can successfully implement a new idea that adds value. We are currently living in an ideas economy which relies on turning ideas into innovation faster than the competition, which is key to business success.

Fresh thinking and innovating are great for our overall wellbeing. We all have the capacity to innovate, and this is something that many of us do through even the smallest improvement we make every day of our lives. Being an innovator may well involve a bit of risk taking, even falling at the first hurdle, however setbacks are merely opportunities in disguise and it's beyond our comfort zone where the real magic happens!

How to be a great innovator

TOP 3 TIPS

1. Be willing to experiment

Experimentation and innovation go hand in hand and a willingness to learn new things and to experiment will open up all sorts of opportunities and avenues for innovation.

2. Be courageous

Courage requires us to face up to what we may be afraid of and then identify what we can do to overcome some of those fears. Often the fear of failure is a barrier to innovation. Failure, however, is an opportunity to learn and some of the greatest innovations fell at the very first hurdle!

3. Celebrate success

Innovation requires skill, time and effort which can result in some of our greatest achievements, so it is important to celebrate our success. This, in turn, will be motivational and encourage us to seek out future ways to innovate.

Summary

This is by no means the definitive list of behavioural skills that we will need for the future; however, these ten core skills have been identified through extensive research and collaboration to provide a useful collection.

The World Economic Forum produces some excellent content around skills for the future and has been a useful resource for researching this book. For more information visit www.weforum.org

If you would like a free copy of the poster over the page or to find out more about the Future Human podcast series that Liggy has developed with Adam Lacey from Assemble You, then please do email

liggy@liggywebb.com

FUTURE HUMAN

How to evolve well and thrive

BE FLEXIBLE

PLAN A
PLAN B
PLAN C

BUILD resilience

? ? ?
Be curious

MANAGE TIME WELL

COLLABORATE WELL WITH OTHERS

EMPATHISE

BE CREATIVE

iNNOVATE

APPLY CRITICAL THINKING

USE INITIATIVE & RESOURCEFULNESS

The point of human evolution is adapting to circumstance

Sonali Bendre

Explore more at: www.liggywebb.com